Nutcracker Ballet
Coloring Book

Brenda Sneathen Mattox

Grace Oman
snow
boy
soldier

Dover Publications, Inc.
Mineola, New York

Publisher's Note

The Nutcracker was first performed in 1892 in St. Petersburg, Russia. It was not seen in the United States until 1944, but it has become extremely popular, especially during the Christmas season, when many dance companies present it to the delight of children everywhere! Who wouldn't like to see a ballet with a trip to the Land of Sweets in a walnut boat, or a battle between a Nutcracker doll and a Mouse King! In some versions of *The Nutcracker,* the little girl's name is Marie, rather than Clara—Marie was the name of the character in E. T. A. Hoffmann's tale "The Nutcracker and the Mouse King," upon which the original ballet was based.

Ballets have been performed in Europe for several hundred years. There are classical ballets, with dancers in flowing gowns and fairy tale stories. Modern ballets have stories that are more realistic, as well as costumes that may be more colorful and less delicate than those of the classics.

The Nutcracker is a classical ballet that never loses its charm. As you read about Clara and her exciting Christmas Eve, you can color in the scenes any way you wish, using colored pencils, crayons, or markers. Enjoy your visit to this land of enchantment!

Bibliographical Note

Nutcracker Ballet Coloring Book is a new work, first published by Dover Publications, Inc., in 2005.

International Standard Book Number

ISBN-13: 978-0-486-44022-4
ISBN-10: 0-486-44022-2

Manufactured in the United States by Courier Corporation
44022206
www.doverpublications.com

The first act of *The Nutcracker* ballet begins on Christmas Eve.
Clara and her brother, Fritz, peer through the doors to
see the adults preparing for the Christmas party.

Papa and Fritz welcome the first guests to the party.

Godpapa Drosselmeyer has arrived, and Mama brings Clara to greet him. He is an inventor who makes marvelous moving toys.

All the children take part in a festive holiday dance.

The boys kneel and clap as the girls whirl around in their wide skirts.

One of Godpapa Drosselmeyer's gifts to Clara's family is this pair of life-sized dolls, Harlequin and Columbine. The dolls dance for the company.

Godpapa's special gift for Clara is a wonderful
nutcracker doll that looks like a soldier.

Fritz is jealous of Clara's gift, and he grabs the Nutcracker and
stomps on it. Clara pulls him away, as the startled guests look on.

The party has ended, and Clara prepares for bed. She has bandaged
the Nutcracker's broken jaw and lovingly puts it in a doll's bed.

That night, Clara dreams that the Christmas tree is growing
taller and taller. Clara seems to be the size of a doll!

From a hole in the wall, the terrifying seven-headed Mouse King appears!

The Nutcracker comes to life and battles the Mouse
King. When it looks as if the Nutcracker will lose, Clara
throws her slipper at the Mouse King, killing him.

After the death of the Mouse King, the Nutcracker removes
the seventh crown and is changed into a handsome prince!

The next scene of the ballet takes place in the Kingdom of Snow.

Lovely Snowflakes take the stage and perform an elegant dance.

Clara and the Prince, riding in a boat made from
a walnut, arrive in the Land of Sweets.

The Sugar Plum Fairy and her angels have been waiting
to welcome Clara and the Prince to her palace.

The Prince and Clara are seated on the Throne of Delight.
They are given all sorts of goodies to eat while they
watch the entertainment planned just for them.

Spanish Hot Chocolate does a lively dance with her
partner, surrounded by all sorts of chocolate treats!

Arabian Coffee leaps around the coffee pot to
the sound of jingling bells and cymbals.

China Tea and her partner, wearing colorful
silk robes, perform a delightful dance.

Peppermint does a lively dance with a great candy hoop.

Lovely Marzipan and her two handmaidens
dance to the sweet tunes of their flutes.

Little Polichinelles, or "Punches," are hidden in the enormous
skirt of comical Mother Ginger. They take the stage to dance.

The delightful "Punches" wait for the last dancer to join their group.

Pretty Dew Drop leads the Waltz of the Flowers.

The beautiful Flowers fill the stage as they perform an exciting waltz.

The Sugar Plum Fairy and her partner dance
together at the end of this marvelous show.

The Sugar Plum Fairy kisses a sleepy Clara
good-bye before the Prince escorts her home.

Clara and the Prince fly away into the night sky in a
magical sleigh drawn by a pair of reindeer.